ULTIMATE
FIELD TRIP

BLASTING OFF TO SPACE ACADEMY

by Susan E. Goodman   photographs by Michael J. Doolittle

ALADDIN PAPERBACKS

NEW YORK   LONDON   TORONTO   SYDNEY   SINGAPORE

TO JAKE,
who has the smarts
and the daring to
make it to Mars
—S.G.

**TO TIM,
TED, JON, AND
MATTHEW—**
the best brothers on
this planet
—M.D.

First Aladdin Paperbacks edition May 2002

Text copyright © 2001 by Susan E. Goodman

Illustrations copyright © 2001 by Michael J. Doolittle

U.S. Space Camp and U.S. Space Academy are registered trademarks of the U.S. Space and Rocket Center.

Aladdin Paperbacks, An imprint of Simon & Schuster, Children's Publishing Division

1230 Avenue of the Americas, New York, NY 10020

Also available in an Atheneum Books for Young Readers hardcover edition.

Designed by Anne Scatto/PIXEL PRESS

The text of this book was set in Monotype Fournier.

Printed in China

10 9 8 7 6 5 4 3 2 1

The Library of Congress has cataloged the hardcover edition as follows:

Goodman, Susan E., 1952-

Ultimate field trip 5 : blasting off to Space Academy / by Susan E. Goodman ;
photographs by Michael J. Doolittle.

p. cm.

Includes bibliographical references.

ISBN 0-689-83044-0 (hc.)

1. Space Academy (U.S. Space Camp (Huntsville, Ala.)—Juvenile literature.

2. Astronauts—Training of—United States—Juvenile literature. 3. Space flight training facilities—
United States—Juvenile literature. 4. School field trips—Juvenile literature.

[1. Space Academy (U.S. Space Camp (Huntsville, Ala.) 2. Astronauts. 3. School field trips.]

I. Title: Blasting off to Space Academy. II. Doolittle, Michael J., ill. III. Title.

TL1085.G654 2001

629.45'07—dc21   00-038082

ISBN: 0-689-84863-3 (Aladdin pbk.)

ACKNOWLEDGMENTS

We'd like to thank the kids and chaperons of the Europa team for letting us tag along with them. All the staff at U.S. Space Academy really helped this book take off. A special thanks to Niki Dean who eased our way, counselors Bethany Himel and Paul Atkinson for their good-natured patience, James Scott for his encyclopedic knowledge, and Ed Davis for his expert review of the manuscript. The people at NASA provided us with many special photographs and Don Heiny and Pete Hvizdak had great insights during the photo review. We are eternally grateful to designer Anne Scatto for this series' signature look. Caitlin Van Dusen, thanks for so ably running interference. And, Marcia Marshall, thanks for everything.

CONTENTS

As tall as a thirty-six-story building, the *Saturn 5* rocket launched the Apollo missions to the Moon. Gathered in and around its thrusters are our Space Academy trainees. Standing from left to right: Jonathan Kegan, Jared Bentley. Seated from left to right: Erin Springer, Shane Flynn, Stephanie Winters, Devin Spencer, Lindsay Teutsch, Stacy Manciero, Charles Cote, Erin Beach, Isabelle Dansereau, Alex Moore, Guillaume Couture, Frank Eslinger, Catherine Cournoyer, and Courtney Kossel.

CHAPTER 1

COUNTDOWN TO ADVENTURE

WHAT'S THE BEST PART of being an astronaut? Is it the thrill of rocketing out of Earth's atmosphere at 25,000 miles per hour? Is it the chance to make new scientific discoveries? Or is it the adventure of leaving the familiar behind and going, as someone once put it, "where no man has gone before?"

Few people actually get to answer these questions by traveling into space. But some kids took the first step by going to U.S. Space Academy at the United States Space and Rocket Center in Huntsville, Alabama.

"I can't tell whether this fits or not," said Shane. "Do I look like an astronaut?" Another kid's comment: "If you have to go to the bathroom quick, these flight suits are a bummer."

For almost a week they used the same simulators that real astronauts use and learned how to walk on the Moon and work without gravity. They built their own rockets and visited the ones scientists used to launch the Apollo astronauts to the Moon. They tried tasting space food and wearing space suits. They learned how to eat in space, sleep in space, even how to go to the bathroom without any gravity.

The Habitat, where kids sleep at Space Academy, was designed as an earthbound space station with stairs and handrails to get from floor to floor. In space, you'd float where you need to go.

During their training they became a team, Team Europa, named after one of Jupiter's seven moons. Then, Europa blasted off on a mission of its own. . . .

CHAPTER 2

ON THE TRAINING FLOOR

"EUROPA, THE TRAINING CENTER is a dirt-free zone," said Paul. "Gum and drinks can create disasters here."

Paul, one of Europa's team leaders, led the kids through a maze of strange-looking machines. As they walked, the kids peeked at other teams jumping high enough to dunk a basketball and spinning in what looked like a giant gyroscope. Paul explained that astronauts trained for years before going into space. It takes lots of practice to learn how to function in such a different environment. On space walks, for example, they must make delicate repairs while floating upside down. In their ships they must learn how to drift rather than walk through the air.

How do they learn these things while anchored by Earth's gravity? To find out, Europa tried some of the simulators that astronauts have used.

THE ⅙ GRAVITY CHAIR

"The Moon has only one-sixth of our gravity," explained Paul. "If you weigh one hundred twenty pounds here, you'd only weigh twenty pounds on the Moon. And you'd have to learn to walk differently because there isn't as much traction."

To practice this movement, the kids used a ⅙ Gravity Chair similar to the Apollo astronauts'. In fact, Europa learned from the astronauts' experiences. The best ways to get around were a slow jog and the bunny hop.

John waited impatiently while Paul adjusted the chair to offset five-sixths of his weight.

"Bunny hop for me," said Paul.

"You've got to be kidding," answered John. "I can barely reach the ground."

Soon, however, he was leaping across the training floor.

"This looks like good practice for the high jump," said Stephanie.

"It shouldn't be; you want to jump for distance, not height," said Paul. "Astronaut Charlie Duke of *Apollo 16* tried to set a height record. But his life-support pack changed his center of gravity. He landed on his back and couldn't get up, just like a beetle. If John Young hadn't been around to help him, he could have been stuck there until *Apollo 17!*"

THE MULTI-AXIS TRAINER (MAT)

"Remove everything from your pockets," said Bethany, Europa's other team leader. "Take off your necklaces, too, so you don't get whacked in the face."

To get ready for the MAT, some kids took off jewelry; others just took a few deep breaths. The MAT looks like an atom gone wild, with each of its three outer circles spinning separately and you as its whirling nucleus. The Mercury astronauts used it to learn how to regain control of a tumbling spacecraft.

The MAT never turns more than twice in the same direction, which is supposed to keep you from feeling sick. That didn't keep a lot of kids from getting nervous. But once they tried it, the glint of silver braces flashed through their smiles.

"It was terrific," said Stacy, "but next time, I'll tie my hair back so it doesn't keep hitting my face."

"It's awesome," Stephanie agreed.

When asked how she'd feel doing it for a ten-minute stretch in a spaceship, Stephanie added, "Your head spins like crazy, but it doesn't feel bad."

"I couldn't help smiling all the time because it was so much fun," said Lindsay.

THE FIVE DEGREES OF FREEDOM (5DF) CHAIR

On Earth, when you jump up, gravity pulls you back down. In space, you just keep going up. If you push away from a wall, you keep going backward. Bending quickly to grab something could make you do somersaults. To get used to the weightless tumble of space, the Gemini and Apollo astronauts—and the kids at Space Academy—used the 5DF Chair. This chair glided over the floor on a cushion of air like the puck in an air hockey game.

"This is what an EVA, an extravehicular activity, or space walk, feels like," Bethany said, tipping and rolling the chair in all direction to give the kids a taste of the different movements.

Bethany held on to the 5DF Chair to keep it safe. In space, astronauts are tethered to their ship. It's a good thing, too. When astronaut Pete Conrad went on his space walk, he lost hold of *Skylab*. That tether was the only thing that kept him from floating away.

In the 5DF Chair, kids practiced inching their way along a wall. Once Lindsay pushed herself away by accident, she had a hard time getting back.

"Swim, Lindsay, swim!" Courtney called out.

Lindsay tried to breaststroke her way back to the wall—it was hopeless.

"Oh, well," said Charles, "she's *Lost in Space!*"

This is the way Frank and most kids feel going up on the Space Shot . . .

SPACE SHOT

"This is your last chance to change your mind," said the operator. "Once the generator has been charged, we cannot stop."

In just seconds, the kids were blasting off on the Space Shot. They would rocket skyward with a force of 4 Gs, one more than astronauts experience during their launches. All that force meant that, for a few seconds at the top, before gravity pulled them back, the kids could feel what it was like to weightless.

NASA doesn't use the Space Shot to simulate weightlessness; it trains astronauts aboard its KC-135 airplane. The plane climbs sharply and then free-falls straight toward the ground, up again, then down again, and again. For twenty-five seconds, at the top of each roller-coaster ride, the plane's passengers are weightless. But many astronauts have paid a price for this amazing experience. The KC-135 is nicknamed the "Vomit Comet" for good reason.

"I wish I hadn't eaten so much breakfast," said Erin S. as she waited for her turn on the Space Shot. "I'm going to scream. It helps you not throw up."

. . . and they feel this way coming down. Devin was amazed that one kid in line thought the experience would cure his fear of heights.

Some people call the Space Shot "an elevator with an attitude."

At least half the astronauts experience space sickness at the beginning of their voyage. That's why John Young didn't do Gus Grissom any favor when he smuggled him a corned beef sandwich on the *Gemini 3* mission. The story is Grissom threw up; in weightless conditions, that's a difficult cleanup job.

Before her second ride, Erin was too excited to feel sick. "I love that feeling of just shooting up there," she said.

"Then you rise up out of your chair and float there for a second," said Stacy. "Weightlessness, I wish it lasted a lot longer."

THE POOL

Another way the earthbound astronauts simulate working in weightlessness is by going underwater. At Houston's Lyndon B. Johnson Space Center, astronauts practice in a huge water tank holding a full-scale model of the Shuttle's payload bay. At Space Academy, the kids went to a swimming pool.

"Your job is to build a cube underwater as fast as possible," said Bethany. "It takes teamwork, an ability to work in weightlessness, and—something astronauts don't need, I hope—an ability to hold your breath."

The water started boiling as kids grabbed

Each strut, or tube, belonged in a specific place.

8

Once the kids started working together, the cube was built quickly.

struts and dove underwater. It kept boiling as they came up for air again and again, slowing realizing they needed a better plan. . . .

"Ten minutes and fifty-six seconds," Bethany said when they finally finished. "Well, every astronaut has to start somewhere. How could you have gone faster?"

"Talk more to each other?" said Isabelle.

"That's right," Bethany agreed. "Communication, letting your leaders lead, and teamwork. It's true in the pool, and it will be even more important when you work to make your own space mission a real success."

AMAZING SPACE FACTS
COUNTDOWN
8...

Flawed when it went into orbit in 1990, the Hubble Space Telescope was repaired in 1993 during a spectacular mission that required five space walks. Located above our hazy atmosphere, the Hubble sees deep into the universe to reveal black holes, new galaxies, the birth of some stars and the death of others. Its "eagle-eyed vision" is so acute that if the Hubble were on Earth, it could spot a firefly ten thousand miles away!

The International Space Station will orbit 220 miles above Earth.

LIVING IN SPACE

"NOT EVERYBODY IN THE space program is an astronaut," said Ron Hathaway. "I'm an engineer and I'm really proud to be working on the Space Station. It's my gift to my grandkids—and our whole society's future."

Ron worked a few miles away at NASA's Marshall Space Flight Center. He came to Space Academy to tell the kids about the new International Space Station (ISS) being built on Earth and assembled in space. The ISS will let scientists study how being in space affects people, materials, and technologies over time. We need this information to plan a successful outpost on the Moon or a trip to Mars.

The people at Marshall Space Flight Center were building the ISS sections where astronauts will work and live. Eventually crews of four or more will spend up to six months

Erin, Courtney, and Catherine tried out the model of the Space Station's shower, toilet, and sleeping station. Catherine knew her arms would be floating in microgravity.

Canadian astronaut Bjarni V. Tryggvason opted for no pillow when he slept on space shuttle *Discovery*.

in the Space Station. Ron showed the kids pictures of the habitation module, which includes a kitchen, bathroom, beds, medical facility, and the exercise equipment necessary to keep muscles strong in a weightless environment or microgravity.

"Everything is so smooshed together," said Alex. "The astronauts will feel cramped."

"Eventually we'll be able to make things bigger. But our new station is still four times bigger than *Mir,* Russia's old one," Ron answered. "Since we carry all the parts up in the Shuttle, they have to fit its payload."

On Earth, few people think about how they perform the tasks of daily life. In a space station, a confined area without gravity, every activity must be considered carefully.

Tired? In space, if not strapped into bed, astronauts could float around and bump into everything. So they either curl up in a sleeping bag attached to a wall or in a sleep station with bunks that look like deep wall shelving. Some astronauts wear an eye-mask because day and night each last only forty-five minutes when orbiting Earth at 17,500 MPH.

Hungry? Astronaut food often comes in plastic pouches that are cut open and squeezed directly into the mouth. Seasoning it isn't so easy—think about using a saltshaker or a pepper mill in space. So scientists have dissolved salt in water that can be squeezed onto food. Since pepper doesn't dissolve, it's put in vegetable oil. To keep it from floating away, food is attached onto a tray with Velcro, which is, in turn, attached onto astronauts' legs.

Dirty? Spitting toothpaste into a sink would be a messy disaster, so NASA developed a nonfoaming variety the astronauts swallow (or spit into a towel). On the Shuttle, astronauts take sponge baths and clean their hair by wiping it with a cloth that's coated with a rinse-free shampoo. On the ISS, they'll shower by soaping up and vacuuming away the suds.

"Water would float all over if we used a shower nozzle," Ron explained. "Besides, astronauts will only be allowed one gallon of water

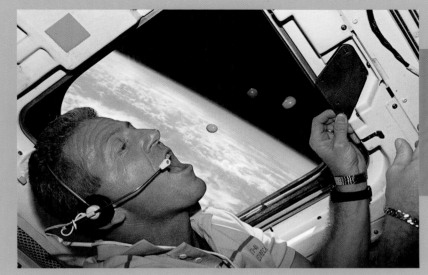

In space, even adults like Loren Shriver can't resist playing with their food.

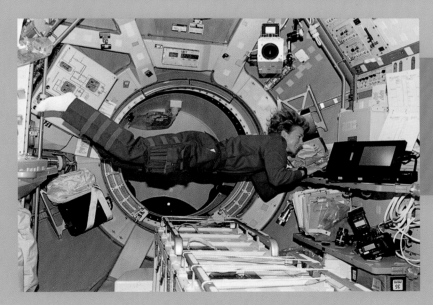

Space is one of the few places where it's okay to "lie down on the job."

Erin takes note of *Apollo 16*'s cramped quarters.

a day for washing. It takes about seventeen thousand dollars to bring a gallon of water into space, so the ISS will only have one hundred gallons that will constantly be recycled."

"Are you saying that they'll drink the water they wash in?" asked Charles.

"Yes," said Ron, "but once it's recycled, it will be cleaner than the water you drink on Earth."

"Shower water seems bad enough," one kid muttered to another. "If they recycle anything else, I'd never go into space." (Sorry, they recycle just about every drop!)

The kids really understood how hard it was to take all these factors into consideration once they began planning their own project. Their assignment was to invent a Mars-based money-making scheme that would help pay to

Several kids wanted to name their project "Operation Moses."

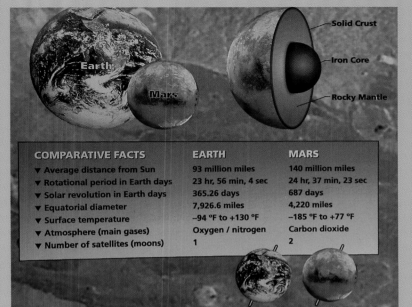

COMPARATIVE FACTS	EARTH	MARS
▼ Average distance from Sun	93 million miles	140 million miles
▼ Rotational period in Earth days	23 hr, 56 min, 4 sec	24 hr, 37 min, 23 sec
▼ Solar revolution in Earth days	365.26 days	687 days
▼ Equatorial diameter	7,926.6 miles	4,220 miles
▼ Surface temperature	−94 °F to +130 °F	−185 °F to +77 °F
▼ Atmosphere (main gases)	Oxygen / nitrogen	Carbon dioxide
▼ Number of satellites (moons)	1	2

colonize the planet. Then they had to build a model of their idea with LEGOs and K'nex.

Kids proposed all sorts of ideas, from mining for minerals to creating a luxury resort with tours to Mars's moons. Erin S. even suggested a Martian branch of Space Academy. Finally they decided to build a complex for sporting events.

"A fine plan," said Bethany, "but you also have to think about the practical side. What will you eat? Are you going to bring up animals? If so, how will you feed them? How can you get enough oxygen?"

"And TV," John said, thinking that life support included more than air and water.

"Where would we plug in a TV?" asked Devin.

"An outlet, of course," John answered.

"Where will the electricity come from?" she asked.

"Details!" said John.

The kids did come up with the idea of trees to supply oxygen and solar

SPACE SCALES
COMPARE YOUR WEIGHT ON THE EARTH, MOON & MARS

Howe Richardson

panels for power. Just as they started to bog down trying to figure out how solar energy translates into electricity, Bethany saved the day. "You will have engineers to do that," she said. "And don't forget the project will take place in the future, so it won't necessarily be limited by the boundaries of current scientific knowledge." That's when Europa's creativity really took off.

The kids were proud of their finished model, which included hovercrafts to travel over Mars's rocky surface, a monorail for touring the planet, and a snowboarding station at Mars's Olympus Mons (the highest peak in the solar system).

Erin S. started building the FlyTime, a system where rockets pass through a wormhole straight to Mars's moon Deimos. From there, a shuttle would transport passengers to the planet itself. Jared began working on a dome for the sports arena. He made it especially tall so the basketball backboards could be set at over twenty feet to compensate for Mars's gravity, which is only three-eighths that of Earth. Other kids constructed domes for living and working and for growing food and animals.

"What are you doing?" Bethany asked when she saw Devin building a wall out of red and yellow LEGOs.

"First things first," said Devin, "I'm making a McDonald's."

BUILDING ROCKETS

BEFORE A LAUNCH, the Shuttle's four main parts are put together in the Vehicle Assembly Building (VAB), near Cape Canaveral in Florida. Its ET (External Tank) alone is half a football field high, so the building has to be huge. In fact, it is so big that when the temperature is hot outside and it's cold inside, clouds form near the ceiling and create rainstorms.

The ET, which provides fuel for the orbiter's engines, becomes the Shuttle's backbone. Attached to its sides are the two SRBs (Solid Rocket Boosters) that also help blast the orbiter into space. Finally the orbiter itself, which holds the crew and their cargo, perches on the ET's back.

"Where are our ET and SRBs?" asked Guillaume, looking through his rocket kit.

"I bet NASA doesn't use Elmer's to put their rockets together," said Jared.

"This rocket might be made of cardboard and plastic, but it can go pretty high if it's built right," Bethany answered.

Then she put the kids to work. "First, put the green rings into the blue tube," she said. "They will hold your engine in place."

"Mine won't go in," said Stephanie.

"Use the Force," said Alex.

Next the kids glued cardboard rings to the outside of the tubes so this engine assembly would fit snugly in the rocket. To make it secure, the kids used glue. Some used a lot of glue.

Bethany explained that the hole in the middle of the parachute made it open better and descend straighter.

"Houston, we have a problem," said Jared. "I have glued myself to the tube."

"At least my rocket won't fall apart," said Lindsay. When she set it down, her model promptly stuck to the paper towel. "I guess I'll be the first to launch paper towels into space," she added.

The kids taped fins onto their rockets' booster stage for stability. After fitting a parachute into its special compartment, they put on the payload section and the nose cone.

"Think this is how they do it at NASA?" Shane asked.

NASA may use more high-tech methods and materials, but all rockets operate on the same principle. Fuel burns hot and fast,

AMAZING SPACE FACTS
COUNTDOWN 5...

Once, urine was ejected from the orbiter while it was in the cold part of its orbit, and the urine froze onto the ship. Mission Control feared this frozen mess might rip the heat tiles off the ship when it re-entered Earth's atmosphere. Yet the astronauts refused to do a space walk to solve the problem because they didn't want to be known as the ones who chipped urine off the Shuttle. They ended up using the remote control Canadarm instead.

Guillaume held his rocket in front of the *Pathfinder*, the Shuttle mock-up made to test whether something so heavy could be lifted by crane and brought to a launchpad.

forming gases that expand and rush out of one end. If the thrust or power is greater than the rocket's weight (the force of gravity), it moves forward. The more thrust in relation to the rocket's weight, the greater its speed. The orbiter's main engines put out the same amount of power as twenty-three Hoover Dams. At liftoff, the Shuttle has over 7.3 million pounds of thrust, enough to take its 5 million pounds up into space. The kids' rockets only weighed about 2 ounces, and 1.7 ounces of thrust was enough to lift them into the sky.

Stephanie had a passenger in her payload bay. When her rocket ended as a "Lawn Dart," Bethany said, "Your alien might have sustained a few injuries on that landing."

Once back in Earth's atmosphere, the Shuttle works like a glider rather than an airplane. The friction of being in Earth's atmosphere slows it down to a safe landing speed.

"I bet mine will never get off the ground," Frank said as the group lined their rockets up on the launchpad.

"When I count down to one," said the instructor, "you push the launch button."

If all went according to plan, once the kids' rockets were high in the sky, a second charge would split their two stages. Their parachutes would pop out so they could gently drift to Earth. The Shuttle works a little differently. Within two minutes of liftoff, the solid rocket boosters that push the orbiter into space break away and parachute back to Earth to be used again. Six minutes later, the ET, now empty, is abandoned and breaks up in the atmosphere. The orbiter circles Earth until it's done with its mission.

Jared's experimental "four-stage" rocket, *Saturn 4*, flew surprisingly high.

Stacy held her breath as she pressed the launch button.

Then the ship slows itself down and lets gravity pull it back toward Earth.

One by one, the kids came out to test their rockets.

"Three, two, one . . ."

Shane pressed the ignite button. His model went straight up, like, well, a rocket. But his parachute didn't open, so it came down like a guided missile. Its nose cone stuck in the ground.

"We call that a 'Lawn Dart,'" said the instructor.

"Three, two, one . . ."

Another confusing launch. "Hey, what was that thing that came out?" asked Stacy.

NASA avoids all sorts of problems by having its booster rockets land in the ocean.

"It would be so neat if the wind blew my rocket all the way to Michigan so my parents could see it," said Stacy.

Catherine retrieved her rocket and looked at the bottom of its tube. "It's all burned," she said, "I guess that means it's a success."

"Sadly, it was your engine," said the instructor.

"Ouch," said Jared, "that hurt."

"Now you know how people at NASA sometimes feel," said Bethany. "It's good training."

"Three, two, one . . ."

Finally a launch and a landing that would make NASA technicians stand up and cheer.

"Well, folks," Courtney said as she went to pick up her rocket, "I may have found a new career!"

A one-stage rocket, the *Redstone*, launched the first U.S. astronaut, Alan Shepard, into space in 1961. Lindsay took one look at this missile in Rocket Park and said, "I wouldn't like to go up in space on that thing."

AMAZING SPACE FACTS
COUNTDOWN
9...

Want to be taller? Go into space. With no gravity to push on their bones, astronauts can "grow" up to two inches while on their missions. Don't get too excited, though. They shrink once they return to Earth's gravity.

CHAPTER 5

WE HAVE LIFTOFF

Mission Control was almost too busy to watch this perfect launch on their screens.

"T MINUS EIGHT MINUTES and counting. All systems are 'go' for an on-time launch of Shuttle *Endeavour,*" Jared said into his headset.

The kids were excited, but nervous. Their mission might not have been real, but it sure felt like it. Each of them had an important part to play—on the ground, in the ship, out in space—to make their simulated journey into space a success.

"Pilot, it's time to start the fuel cells," reported Stacy. Stacy was the Capcom, the only person at Mission Control who talked to *Endeavour*'s crew. In real life,

These kids represented the hundreds of people at Mission Control in Huntsville, in Houston, and in Florida.

the Capcom is always an astronaut so she or he knows firsthand what the crew is experiencing. Stacy sat with Jared and the four other kids of Mission Control who operated computers, gave advice, and monitored every aspect of the flight.

"The fuel cells have started," said Erin B., the person in charge of spacecraft systems.

"We are switching to internal power," she finished reading as she flipped some switches on her console.

Erin and the rest of the team had scripts that told them what to do and when. But not everything was preplanned—as they soon found out. Just a few minutes before launch, a red light flashed across Mission Control's computer screens. It signaled a problem with the power source that helped move *Endeavour*'s engines and fins.

"We have a problem," announced Catherine, the Flight Director.

A computer screen that helps the kids at Mission Control monitor every detail of the Shuttle flight.

"It was exciting when we went into orbit," said Frank. "The ship jolted so much that my headphones flew off."

26

"I'm on it," Erin B. said, racing to find the computer code that would fix it.

"We only have a few more seconds," warned Catherine.

"Got it," cried Erin B.—and just in time.

"Ten . . . nine . . . eight . . ."

On their computer screens, clouds of smoke began pouring out of the Shuttle's engines.

"Seven . . . six . . . five . . ."

Five Europa astronauts sat strapped into the *Endeavour* simulator. They were tilted into a launch position. Its speakers rumbled with the roar of the engines.

"Two . . . one . . . we have liftoff!" Mission Control said over their radio.

Endeavour's crew hardly needed this announcement. The simulator bolted and shook, its screens showing a blue sky turning darker and darker until it became space.

Meanwhile, in the Space Station, Stephanie and Devin began suiting up to repair the Hubble Space Telescope. To counteract the heat of a heavy space suit, NASA's astronauts wear garments near their skin that circulate cold water through plastic tubes. The astronauts at Space

AMAZING SPACE FACTS
COUNTDOWN
3...

NASA's first space suits were silver colored. They only protected Mercury astronauts if their capsule depressurized. Today's version shields astronauts from space's deadly environment and keeps them comfortable. An astronaut can get hungry working in space, so the suit has a granola bar mounted at the shoulder along with a straw for water. The other shoulder has an emery board to scratch an itchy nose. A stream of air flows from the top of the suit to below the neck to keep the effects of sneezes and space sickness from blocking an astronaut's vision.

"I feel like a robot," said Devin. "Space suits have to be strong," Bethany told her. "Tiny micro-meteorites are like 'space bullets' and, if they could pierce your suit, you'd have a few problems."

27

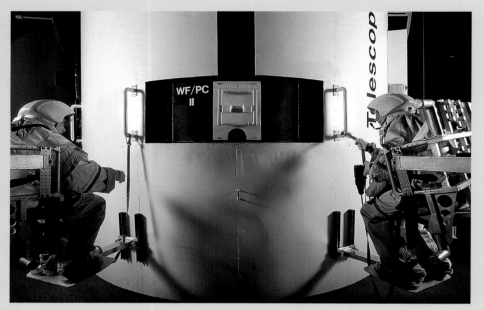

Academy wore ice packs. Stephanie felt cold until she attached her version of a space suit's LTU (Lower Torso Unit) to her boots and put the HUT (Hard Upper Torso) over her head. The girls strapped themselves into 5DF Chairs to simulate the floating freedom of weightlessness. They put on earphones to communicate with each other and Mission Control. Teetering back and forth and side to side, they slid on cushions of air to the Hubble.

The real Hubble, which has given us amazing information about our universe, is run by chips so old, they couldn't run many of today's computer games.

Their first job—to tether themselves to the Hubble so they wouldn't drift off. Their second: to replace the telescope's battery and computer cartridge—quite a challenge when wearing thick, space-proof gloves and sitting in a device that glided away if you so much

Cordless drills were first invented for the Apollo astronauts to use on the Moon. It was easier than making an extension cord that was long enough.

as bent forward. Stephanie tried unscrewing the bolt on the telescope with one hand while hanging on with the other.

"Uh-oh, I lost the screw. I guess it just floated away," she said, getting into the microgravity spirit of things. "Now, I'm floating away. I'm sure glad we're tethered."

Safely in orbit 176.3 miles above Earth, the mission specialist on *Endeavour* opened the payload doors to rid the orbiter of built-up heat. Then they prepared to deploy a satellite for cable TV. They only had a fifteen-second window to release the satellite. Any earlier or later, and as Mission Control explained it, "The satellite would be out of position. We'd have an angry company and a lot of people enjoying free cable in Antarctica."

"Commander, we have a 'go' for the predeploy maneuver," said Capcom Stacy.

"Roger that," Courtney said as she turned to the orbiter's incredible combination of switches, joysticks, and computer screens.

"I had so many buttons to push," said Courtney, "and I could barely reach them."

With only twelve seconds to go, Courtney finally spoke into her headset. "All pre-deployment procedures complete. We are a 'go,' Mission Control."

Pilot Frank deployed the satellite right on schedule. Immediately he began moving *Endeavour* away so it wouldn't be damaged when an engine fired to push the satellite into its orbit.

Nine minutes later, when Mission Control announced that the satellite was transmitting a strong signal (to the

Gravity causes many materials to separate because heavier elements sink to the bottom. Scientists think making certain materials in microgravity will improve them. Charles conducted his own experiment—in gravity, of course. But he used the same techniques as astronauts in space do to create a substance that bounced like rubber.

right country!), the Shuttle crew was already working on their next assignment.

🪐

In the Space Station, scientists were using test tubes and tape measures to study how microgravity affects chemicals and human bodies. Suddenly a warning signal bathed the room in a flashing red light. Station Commander Erin S. read a downlink that came in from Mission Control.

"Marshall Space Flight Center says a meteor shower is coming our way," she announced. "It should reach the station in three minutes. We must take cover in the air lock—now!"

🪐

Thousands of miles away, it was time for *Endeavour*'s mission specialists to get into their space suits. In NASA-speak, they would construct an EASE on their EVA. In other words, they were building a pyramid in space.

Soon John was twenty-five feet in the air, strapped into an MMU (Manned Maneuvering Unit) simulator. The real MMU is a gas-

Station commander Erin S. emerged from the air lock when the meteor shower had passed.

powered backpack that lets astronauts move around in space without a tether. John's was a chair attached to a long mechanical arm he could move with a joystick. Just like the other two specialists seated in 5DF Chairs, John rolled and swayed as the MMU responded to any of his movements.

John dropped a line, and Guillaume hooked it to one of the pyramid's arms. John hauled the arm up and locked it into place. Down went the line again—this time, a little more quickly than expected.

"Hey, we're not really in space, we have gravity here," said Guillaume. "Don't kill us before we complete our mission."

The three of them struggled on, pushing arms into position only to glide away because of their microgravity chairs. Finally they guided the last arm into place and clicked it in.

"Back to the orbiter," said Guillaume.

"Wait a second," called John, "how do I get down from here?"

NASA astronauts did a similar EASE experiment in the Shuttle payload bay.

"This is awesome, but hard," said one specialist. "You want to be in one place, but the chair wants you to be in another."

AMAZING SPACE FACTS
COUNTDOWN
2...

Talk about hot? The orbiter reentering our atmosphere goes so fast that the friction caused by rubbing against the air heats its exterior to 2,300 degrees Fahrenheit.

Once the danger from meteors had passed, it was back to science at the Space Station. The kids worked on experiments about body changes in space. Without gravity, the body's fluids shift upward rather than stay down low as they do on

Earth. Astronauts end up with puffy faces and skinny legs, called the "chicken legs of space." But this shift does more than make astronauts look funny. It also changes their blood pressure and heart rate and reduces the amount of bodily fluids. Scientists must help astronauts adjust if they are to remain in space for long periods of time.

Since the kids were really in gravity-bound Alabama, they produced this shift a different way. A special bench tipped Shane until his legs were higher than his head. When Erin first measured his ankle, it was eleven inches in diameter. After four minutes, she measured it again. "Oh, gosh," she said, "it has already shrunk a quarter of an inch."

During this experiment, candy fell out of Shane's pocket onto the floor. "Now it's dirty," he said regretfully. "If there wasn't any gravity, it would have just floated and I could gulp it down later."

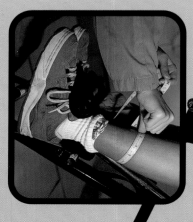

Not having NASA space suits that protected astronauts in temperatures from minus 250 to 250 degrees Fahrenheit, the kids sweated up a storm.

During crises, minutes felt like hours, but all too soon *Endeavour* had to head home. At Mission Control, Jared studied the weather conditions and recommended the John F. Kennedy Space Center in Florida as the best landing site. After hearing from all her experts, Flight Director Catherine okayed moving *Endeavour* into deorbit. Frank began decreasing his ship's speed almost ten thousand miles from the landing site so it would fall out of orbit. About five thousand miles from the site, *Endeavour* entered Earth's atmosphere at more than 16,700 MPH.

      That morning, Paul had reminded the kids that a mission succeeds because of teamwork. By now, Europa was truly a team. The Launch Director figured out how much the

Later, the counselor in the Mission Control room said, "Well done, Europa. I almost thought I was in Florida watching a real launch!"

pilot should adjust the speed brake. Weather and Tracking computed the crosswind blowing near the landing strip. The Spacecraft Systems Officer reported that the orbiter's landing gear was down and locked.

And when Courtney and Frank set *Endeavour* down safely, the cheers were so loud they may have heard them all the way down the road at Marshall Space Flight Center.

CHAPTER 6

MISSION COMPLETED

IN ONE SENSE, the kids graduated when they completed their successful mission. But on their last day, they had an official ceremony with all the other kids who attended U.S. Space Academy that week.

When it was time for the Europa teammates to get their diplomas, Bethany was there to congratulate them. "I had the pleasure of being with this team this week," she said, "and I don't think I've ever had a better one. You worked together and learned a lot. I'll never forget you."

The kids knew they wouldn't forget their experience at U.S. Space Academy, either.

"I'll never forget the counselors and the new kids I met here," said Devin.

"And I won't forget that if you don't put your two-stage rocket together carefully, it will never separate," said John.

"The badge makes me feel different, better than I normally do," said Shane.

COUNTDOWN 1...

You don't have to be an astronaut to benefit from NASA technology. Discoveries made for the space program have improved all our lives. The first disposable diaper wasn't designed for babies—it was a way to deal with the human waste in space. The gel inserts that make sneakers so comfy were made so Apollo astronauts could walk on the Moon's rocky surface. Other NASA spin-offs include scratch-resistant lenses in glasses, football helmet padding, freeze-dried foods, satellite TV technology, lightweight metal in braces, Mylar balloons, expanding foam insulation, and the technology to label on plastic.

Europa won the Outstanding Team Award for having the best cooperation and team spirit.

James, the counselor who ran their mission, wanted them to remember something else. "Many people think that launches begin and end with a pilot and a commander," he said. "Kids come here and realize how many essential roles they can play. I always hope they leave here thinking they don't have to be a pilot to make a difference—or, to be in the space program."

"I do understand a lot more about what it takes to get into space," said Stacy.

"Yeah," said Alex. "I ended up liking being the SSO because I was controlling everything."

"Not everything," said Jared. "I was Weather and Tracking. I did the OMS burn to get *Endeavour* into orbit. They depended on me, too."

At this point in their space careers, however, the kids thought more about what it would be like in space than in Mission Control.

"I've always wanted to fly like a bird," said Alex. "I guess floating in space is the closest I'll ever get."

"I wouldn't mind working here at Space Academy," said Stacy, "but I'd never go up in space. That's too scary."

"I'd like to know what it's like to float and to feel seven Gs and to look back at Earth from hundreds of miles away," said Jared. "Maybe all that is worth being scared."

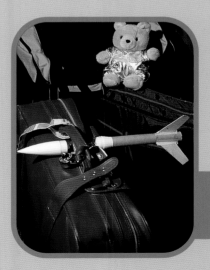

To get back home, some kids had to fly all the way to Quebec, Canada.

GLOSSARY

AIR LOCK—an airtight room used to help people pass safely from one environment to another

ATMOSPHERE—the air and gases that surround Earth and protect it from the Sun's harmful rays and from meteorites

CANADARM—the Shuttle's robot arm, built by Canada, located in its payload bay to help astronauts work outside in space

CAPCOM—the person at Mission Control who communicates with the Shuttle crew

CAPE CANAVERAL—home of the John F. Kennedy Space Center on Florida's coast and NASA's primary launch site

COLONIZE—to make a new settlement or community

CONSOLE—an instrument panel

CROSSWIND—a wind blowing across a runaway that, if strong enough, will create problems

DEPLOY—to remove something from a stowed position and put it into operation

DEPRESSURIZE—to release the atmosphere from a container

DOWNLINK—a way to send data from Earth to a vehicle in space and back

EVA (EXTRAVEHICULAR ACTIVITY)—NASA's term for an astronaut's journey outside a spacecraft

ET (EXTERNAL TANK)—the big tank that carries the fuel for the Shuttle's main engines during launch and ascent

G—the measure of gravity's pull; one G is the force of gravity on Earth

GLIDER—an aircraft without an engine, designed to glide on air currents

HABITATION MODULE—a separate unit of a spacecraft or space station to be lived in

HEAT TILES—tiles made to protect the Shuttle orbiter from the heat of reentering the Earth's atmosphere

HOVERCRAFT—a vehicle that travels over land or water on a cushion of air

LIFE-SUPPORT SYSTEM—equipment that provides an environment in which life can survive

MICROGRAVITY—a condition in which the effects of gravity are greatly reduced

MISSION CONTROL—the network of NASA experts, usually at Johnson Space Center, that help coordinate the orbiter's activities during a mission

MONORAIL—a railway system where the cars hang from a single track

NASA—the National Aeronautics and Space Administration, the agency in charge of the U.S. space program

NOSE CONE—a shield that fits over or is the pointed
   end of a spacecraft
OMS (ORBITAL MANEUVERING SYSTEM)—
   the two engines on the orbiter that provide the power
   to change the orbit
ORBITER—the airplanelike part of the Shuttle that
   goes into space
SIMULATORS—machines used to simulate
   conditions astronauts experience in space
SRBs (SOLID ROCKET BOOSTERS)—
   the two thin rockets attached to the
   Shuttle's ET that provide power for the
   Shuttle's first two minutes of launch and
   ascent
TETHER—a line that attaches the astronauts
   to their spacecraft when they are outside the ship
THRUST—the force that moves a rocket forward
   in reaction to the rushing of exhaust gases out
   of its rear end
VAB (VEHICLE ASSEMBLY BUILDING)—
   the building where the Shuttle is assembled
WEIGHTLESSNESS—a condition in which
   the effects of gravity are greatly reduced
WORMHOLE—an opening that connects
   one part of the universe to another

BIBLIOGRAPHY

Nonfiction books about Space Travel

Dyson, Marianne J. *Space Station Science: Life in Free Fall*. New York: Scholastic, 1999.

Ride, Sally, and Susan Okie. *To Space and Back*. Paperback edition. New York: Lothrop
  Lee & Shepard, 1989.

Scott, Elaine, and Margaret Miller. *Adventure in Space: The Flight to Fix the Hubble*. New
  York: Hyperion Paperbacks for Children, 1995.

Fiction about Space Travel or Space Camp

Card, Orson Scott. *Ender's Game*. Paperback edition. New York: Tor Books, 1994.

Steele, Alexander. *The SUPER Adventures of Wishbone: Unleashed in Space*. Paperback
  edition. Allen, Texas: Lyrick Publishing, 1999.

For information about U.S. Space Academy, contact:

U.S. Space and Rocket Center

P. O. Box 070015

Huntsville, AL 35807-7015

1-800-63-SPACE

Web: www.spacecamp.com